Original title:
The Deer's Song

Copyright © 2024 Swan Charm

Author: Liina Liblikas
ISBN HARDBACK: 978-9908-52-380-4
ISBN PAPERBACK: 978-9908-52-381-1
ISBN EBOOK: 978-9908-52-382-8

The Lyrical Heart of the Forest

In shadows deep where soft winds sigh,
The trees wear crowns of twinkling lights.
A chorus rises, joyful and high,
Nature's dance ignites the nights.

Beneath the stars, the fireflies gleam,
While laughter echoes through the glade.
The forest hums with a vibrant dream,
A tapestry of joy displayed.

Each leaf a song, each branch a cheer,
The whispers blend with the cool night's air.
We gather close, surrounded here,
In harmony, our hearts laid bare.

So let us twirl until the dawn,
With every heartbeat, love renews.
In the lyrical heart, we are reborn,
As festive colors paint our views.

In Tune with the Earth's Breath

The sun spills gold on fields so wide,
Buds burst open, each bloom a song.
The world awakes, no need to hide,
In gentle rhythms, we belong.

With every step on warming ground,
The laughter of nature floats above.
In every whisper, joy is found,
To dance in circles, hand in glove.

The brook babbles secrets, sweet and clear,
While branches sway to the softest tunes.
Together, we'll conjure summer's cheer,
Under the gaze of silver moons.

In this embrace, all worries cease,
Each heartbeat echoes the livelong mirth.
We celebrate life, revel in peace,
In tune with the earth's joyous breath.

The Stillness of Ancestral Paths

In the breezy whispers of the trees,
Echoes of laughter dance with ease,
Beneath the stars, tales unfold,
In a warmth that's timeless, bright, and bold.

Candles flicker, hearts ignite,
With joy and tales shared through the night,
Every step on this sacred ground,
Is a song of heritage, profound.

Gathered souls in festive cheer,
Embracing memories we hold dear,
Woven stories bind us tight,
In this stillness, everything feels right.

With every heartbeat, a joyful sound,
We cherish the love that knows no bound,
In the glow of ancient light,
We celebrate our ancestral might.

Fleeting Glimpses of Wilderness

The forest sings with vibrant leaps,
As laughter hides where wildlife sleeps,
Golden leaves in a waltz, so bright,
Whispers of nature take flight.

Every moment, a treasure found,
In the rustling leaves, joy is unbound,
Sunlight dances on the stream,
In this wild place, we dare to dream.

With echoes of creatures soft and low,
Glimmers of twilight start to glow,
In the stillness, we raise a toast,
To the beauty we cherish the most.

With every heartbeat, life unfolds,
In these fleeting glimpses, stories told,
Underneath the canvas of the sky,
We revel in nature, you and I.

An Ode to the Unseen

In shadows cast where spirits play,
Whispers of joy in the light of day,
We raise our eyes to realms unknown,
In silence, their magic is shown.

From the corners of our hearts, we find,
The unseen forces that bind mankind,
A gentle nudge, a guiding star,
In every soul, they leave a scar.

Through festive nights, we celebrate,
The mysteries held within fate,
With laughter echoing through the dark,
In their embrace, we leave a mark.

So here's to those we cannot see,
In this joyous revelry, we are free,
A toast to the whispers of the night,
In the unseen, we find our light.

Steps in the Harvest Glow

Golden fields beneath a setting sun,
Laughter and joy, the harvest begun,
With every step on this vibrant land,
We gather blessings, hand in hand.

With baskets full of nature's best,
Our hearts are light, our spirits blessed,
The festive air, a sweet embrace,
In this moment, we find our place.

Together we dance with the autumn breeze,
Embracing the gifts that nature frees,
In the glow of twilight, we sing,
Celebrating all that the harvest brings.

With every laugh, with every cheer,
We honor the bounty, year by year,
In this festive gathering, love will flow,
As we tread softly in the harvest glow.

Heartbeats in the Mist

Dancing lights in the twilight glow,
Laughter mingles with the breeze's flow.
Joyful hearts in a vibrant feast,
Celebration blooms, a radiant beast.

Candles flicker, shadows play,
Whispers of magic, come what may.
Colors burst in the evening's air,
Every moment, simply rare.

Elegy for the Lost Clearing

Amidst the trees, a silence falls,
Yet echoes of laughter gently call.
Memories linger in the cooling light,
A festive spirit, pure delight.

In wistful glances, shadows remain,
A dance of joy, tinged with pain.
Nature sings; though some have strayed,
In hearts, their song shall never fade.

Timeless Trails of the Timberlands

Winding paths where the whispers sing,
Leaves rustle softly, as the night takes wing.
Stars appear, a twinkling show,
Adventure waits in moonlit glow.

Gathered round, a fire's warm light,
Friends unite on this cozy night.
The laughter swells like a joyous tide,
In these moments, our hearts confide.

Woodland Reverie

Under the sky, where dreams entwine,
Nature's canvas, a sight divine.
Bubbles of joy in the twilight air,
A festive cheer, beyond compare.

Branches sway in the gentle breeze,
Harmony sings through rustling leaves.
With every heartbeat, reflections bloom,
In the woodland gleam, there's no room for gloom.

Breath of the Wild

In fields where laughter dances bright,
Joyful hearts take joyous flight,
Colorful blooms in the sunlit air,
Nature's canvas, beyond compare.

The breeze carries songs of delight,
Whispers of magic, pure and light,
Under the trees, friendships grow,
In this wild world, love's gentle flow.

Stars twinkle in the velvet sky,
As dreams awaken, spirits fly,
Together under the silvery glow,
In the wild's embrace, we ebb and flow.

With joyous hearts and hands held tight,
We celebrate through day and night,
In nature's arms, forever free,
The breath of the wild is home to me.

Chronicles of the Verdant Groves

Once upon a time in the lush green,
Where laughter echoed, sweet and keen,
The trees held tales of joy and cheer,
In every leaf, a memory dear.

Meadows rich with colors bold,
Happiness in stories told,
Children's laughter danced on air,
As sunlight played without a care.

Breezes carried secrets low,
Murmurs of the earth's soft glow,
In groves where friendships intertwine,
Every moment feels divine.

When twilight comes, the fireflies gleam,
In the dusk, we share our dream,
Together we weave the night's embrace,
Chronicles of joy in this sacred space.

Mother Moon's Gentle Voice

Beneath the stars, she softly sings,
A lullaby that sweetly brings,
Her silver glow, a guiding light,
Bidding us to share the night.

In warm embrace, we find our place,
With every wish, we trace her face,
The moonlit dance of hearts entwined,
In her glow, true love we find.

The night is filled with laughter bright,
Under her gaze, the world feels right,
With every whisper, hope takes flight,
In her presence, spirits ignite.

As stars adorn the velvet sky,
We dream and laugh, together high,
For Mother Moon's embrace is rare,
Her gentle voice fills the night air.

Sylvan Whispers at Dawn

In the hush where day awakes,
Nature stirs, the silence breaks,
Whispers hint of the day ahead,
As sunlight paints the world in red.

Birds take flight on wings so free,
Songs of joy call out to me,
In the glades, a magic found,
Sylvan whispers swirl around.

Morning dew on petals glows,
A symphony of life bestows,
With laughter shared and hands held near,
The dawn invites us to draw near.

In every step, a festive vibe,
Connection flows in every tribe,
As dawn unfolds, our spirits rise,
In nature's dance, we claim the skies.

Gleaming Eyes in the Dusk

As the sun takes its bow, shadows play,
Laughter dances on the breeze, what a day!
Twinkling lights adorn the trees, aglow,
Gleaming eyes sparkle, with festive flow.

Children's joy rings like bells in the air,
Magic weaves through the twilight rare.
With every whisper beneath the stars,
Dreams take flight, like fireflies from afar.

The Call of the Meadow's Heart

In the meadow where daisies sway and twirl,
Festive colors ignite and unfurl.
The laughter of friends echoes wide,
Nature's embrace is where hearts bide.

Sweet scents drift, of harvest's delight,
Gathering warmth beneath moonlight bright.
The night sky hums a soft, soothing tune,
While joy blooms, glowing like the moon.

A Melody in the Underbrush

Rustling leaves whisper secrets of cheer,
Songs of the forest, for all souls to hear.
Glistening trails of starlit dreams,
Twine through the night, in soft silver beams.

Every chirp, every croon, a joyful lore,
The underbrush pulses, calling for more.
Wings flutter and dance, a jubilant flight,
Painting the canvas of the enchanting night.

Sylvan Secrets Unraveled

Among the trees where shadows entwine,
Festive spirits dance, a sigh so divine.
With hearts wide open, we share the glow,
In sylvan secrets, our laughter flows.

The bonfire crackles, stories take flight,
Beneath a tapestry of stars so bright.
Joy is a beacon, guiding us near,
In these woods, we celebrate with cheer.

Traces of Solitude

In the quiet corners of our minds,
Whispers of laughter gently find,
Embers glowing, warmth ignites,
A dance of shadows, pure delight.

Balloons float high, colors in the air,
Each heartbeat echoes love and care,
Hushed moments wrapped in gentle light,
Together we bask in the soft twilight.

Reverie in the Glimmering Grass

Beneath the stars, we lie so low,
With dreams that glisten, like silver glow,
The breeze carries songs of old,
In this embrace, our stories unfold.

Daisies nod in the evening's hum,
As distant laughter begins to come,
Fireflies dance in a rhythmic play,
In this moment, the world melts away.

The Last Light of Daybreak

Crimson hues paint the waking sky,
Joyful whispers, as days pass by,
With every ray, new hopes arise,
We chase the sun, where magic lies.

Gathered round, with friends so dear,
Laughter echoes, voices clear,
A tapestry woven of light and cheer,
Together as one, no hint of fear.

Trails of Enchantment

Paths adorned with daisies bright,
Each step forward, pure delight,
The scent of blossoms fills the air,
In every heartbeat, love and care.

Twinkling lights upon the trees,
Whispers carried on the breeze,
In this magic, we all play,
A festive glow in every way.

Nature's Gentle Rhapsody

Beneath the golden sunlit sky,
The flowers dance, they sway and sigh.
A symphony of color bright,
In harmony, they bloom with light.

The gentle breeze sings soft and low,
While butterflies put on a show.
Birds chirp their joyous, sweet refrain,
In this pure haven, peace remains.

Green leaves rustle, whispers shared,
Nature's secrets, gently bared.
With laughter in the air we roam,
In every corner, we feel at home.

As twilight paints the sky in gold,
A tapestry of dreams unfold.
With every heartbeat, joy we find,
In Nature's rhapsody, entwined.

Ballad of the Wandering Fawn

In the meadow, soft and wide,
A wandering fawn walks with pride.
Her coat a canvas, brown and white,
She dances gently in the light.

Beneath the shade of ancient trees,
She grazes while the warm wind frees.
The world around her sings of cheer,
As crickets chirp, and friends draw near.

With eyes like pools of tranquil grace,
She roams the woods, a secret place.
The soft earth cradles her small feet,
In nature's realm, pure joys repeat.

At dusk, the stars begin to peek,
In velvet skies, their brilliance streaks.
The fawn lays down, her heart content,
Wrapped in blessings, heaven-sent.

Sylvannocturne

As twilight slips on silken threads,
The forest hums, and daylight spreads.
A symphony of night takes flight,
With moonbeams dancing in the light.

The owls call in muted tones,
And shadows play on ancient stones.
While laughter drifts through leafy halls,
As night reveals its wondrous calls.

A brook babbles soft and clear,
In this embrace, we have no fear.
With each rustle and soft sigh,
The whispering night bids time goodbye.

Stars twinkle like a thousand dreams,
In every glance, a world redeems.
Sylvannocturne, our hearts unite,
In nature's arms, all's pure delight.

Secrets in the Underbrush

Beneath the canopy of green,
Lie stories whispered, yet unseen.
The underbrush, a treasure trove,
Where secrets dwell, and wild things rove.

With every step, the earth does speak,
Of timeless tales that nature seeks.
A rustle here, a shadow there,
In hidden nooks, the world lays bare.

Fireflies blink like stars in flight,
Illuminating the velvet night.
Among the roots, where shadows nest,
Life breathes in stillness, at its best.

In this realm, where wonders lay,
Adventure calls, come join the play.
With open hearts, we walk and trust,
To seek the secrets in the brush.

Ethereal Skips and Bounds

In the meadow, laughter flows,
Children dance where sunshine glows,
Bubbles float, a shimmering sight,
Joyful hearts take wing in flight.

Colors burst in vibrant hues,
Nature sings, the world renews,
Music whispers through the trees,
Gentle breezes carry ease.

Stars awaken in twilight's grace,
Dreamy smiles, a soft embrace,
As the moon begins to rise,
Magic sparkles in the skies.

With each skip, with each bound,
Ethereal joys abound,
Festive tones, so sweetly found,
In our hearts, forever crowned.

Harbinger of the Wild

Echoes dance through forest deep,
Where the ancient secrets sleep,
Crisp leaves crunch beneath our feet,
Nature's song, a wild heartbeat.

Creatures peep from shadows nigh,
Underneath a starlit sky,
Windswept laughter fills the air,
Join the rhythm, shed your care.

Harvest moons and glowing beams,
Weave together midnight dreams,
Circles dance in joy's embrace,
Every spirit finds its place.

To the wild, we raise a cheer,
Festivals with friends held dear,
In the woods, we thrive and run,
As the night merges with sun.

Nature's Poised Performance

A stage set with branches wide,
Nature's art, where dreams collide,
Crickets chirp, a rhythmic beat,
Life unfolds in purest heat.

Fireflies twinkle, lights aglow,
Whispers soft, sweet winds that flow,
Every leaf a work of heart,
Nature's poised, a master's art.

Under stars, a grand ballet,
Pulsing night and twilight's play,
Each heartbeat sways, alive with cheer,
Echoed laughs are music here.

As the world joins in the dance,
Take a breath, embrace the chance,
With each step, the magic blooms,
In nature's spell, the spirit zooms.

A Tapestry of Woodland Dreams

In the woods, where shadows gleam,
Eco visions softly beam,
Threads of light through branches weft,
Tapestry of dreams, love's heft.

Winding paths where laughter swells,
Each new story nature tells,
Swaying blooms and vibrant hues,
Fragrant air, a sweet muse's clues.

Gather 'round as fireflies glow,
Underneath the moon's soft show,
Hold your loved ones, share a jest,
In this moment, we are blessed.

Festive hearts in harmony,
Nature's magic, wild and free,
In the tapestry, we weave,
A woodland dream we all believe.

Dance of the Forest Spirits

In moonlight's glow, they swirl and sway,
With laughter bright, they greet the day.
Leaves whisper secrets, the night is young,
To nature's tune, their hearts are sung.

Mushrooms sparkle like jewels of light,
As fireflies twinkle, a dazzling sight.
Among the trees, they spin in glee,
The forest alive with pure harmony.

Serenade of the Fawn

In dew-kissed grass, a soft refrain,
The fawn sings sweet in golden grain.
With gentle steps, she dances near,
Her joyful song, the world can hear.

The sun spills warmth on every flower,
While shadows play in twilight hour.
A serenade of nature's grace,
In this sweet haven, time leaves no trace.

Twilight's Gentle Stroll

Beneath the sky where dusk ignites,
The colors blend like warm delights.
With every step, the stars awake,
A magical path, the night we take.

Whispers of breezes wrap us tight,
Guiding us through the gentle night.
Hand in hand, we softly tread,
With dreams to weave and words unsaid.

Beneath the Canopy's Embrace

The branches dance in the evening breeze,
Sheltering us beneath the leaves.
Nature's warmth in every sigh,
A tranquil song as the night draws nigh.

With twilight's glow, our spirits rise,
As laughter mingles with twilight skies.
In this embrace, we find our place,
In the heart of the woods, a sacred space.

Pathways of the Heartwood

Beneath the boughs, where laughter plays,
The sunlight dances through the leaves,
Each step we take, a joyful phrase,
In nature's chorus, our heart believes.

Flowers bloom in vibrant cheer,
A pathway paved with dreams anew,
Together here, there's naught to fear,
In this embrace, just me and you.

Whispering Pines

The pines sway gently with the breeze,
Their whispers tell of days gone by,
In this forest, hearts find ease,
With every rustle, love draws nigh.

Beneath their arms, we weave our tales,
Of laughter, hope, and starlit skies,
In echoes soft, the spirit sails,
Through fragrant woods, where magic lies.

Listening Skies

Underneath the vast expanse,
The dusk blushes in colors bright,
With every star, a silken dance,
We gather dreams that take their flight.

The moon hums softly, drawing near,
As twilight paints the world with glee,
In these moments, nothing's clear,
Yet hearts unite, wild and free.

Whispers Through the Woodland

Amidst the trees, a gentle song,
Flows with the streams, so pure and clear,
Together here, where we belong,
Nature's rhythm, drawing near.

Hushed conversations in the glade,
As fireflies dance in evening's glow,
In every shadow, dreams are made,
With whispers soft, we let love flow.

Echoes of Graceful Antlers

Upon the hill, the deer do roam,
With antlers high, they claim the night,
In their majestic, quiet home,
We find our souls in nature's light.

Their echoes linger in the air,
Reminding us of paths we tread,
In every glance, a moment rare,
In woods alive, where magic's bred.

Tendrils of Serenity

In twilight's glow, the lanterns sway,
Whispers of joy dance in the fray.
Colors burst on the gentle breeze,
Laughter weaves through rustling leaves.

Stars emerge, the night awakes,
Sweet melodies as laughter breaks.
Hands entwined, the world feels right,
In the embrace of a warm, soft night.

Flowers bloom in a radiant show,
Under the moon's silvery glow.
Each heartbeat flows with a vibrant tune,
Nature rejoices, under the moon.

Together we stand, hearts alight,
Wrapped in warmth, pure delight.
In this moment, all worries cease,
Tendrils of serenity, our sweet peace.

An Evensong of Hidden Trails

Through leafy woods, a soft path calls,
Whispers of magic with ancient thralls.
Sunbeams dance on the dew-kissed grass,
Time slows down as the moments pass.

Birds sing sweet in harmonious flight,
Nature's canvas, a stunning sight.
Every step a promise of cheer,
In hidden trails, all is clear.

The brook babbles a jovial tune,
Under the watch of the glowing moon.
With every turn, the world unfolds,
Secrets of joy in stories told.

So let us wander, hearts entwined,
In evensongs, the peace we find.
Together we roam, hand in hand,
A celebration in this dreamy land.

Nature's Veiled Harmony

In the forest's heart, a symphony plays,
Whispers of trees in a golden haze.
Wildflowers bloom, a vibrant display,
Colors merging in a gentle ballet.

The stream flows gently, a soothing song,
Carrying dreams where we belong.
Each note resonates, a tender chord,
In nature's arms, our spirits soared.

Clouds drift lazily, a painter's brush,
Capturing moments in a tranquil hush.
Sunset kisses the horizon bright,
A canvas alive, spilling pure light.

Harmony dwells where our laughter twirls,
In nature's cradle, our joy unfurls.
Together we bask in this sweet embrace,
Nature's veiled harmony, a sacred space.

Dreams of Springtime in Autumn

Leaves of gold underfoot, a dancing swirl,
Amidst the chill, our hearts unfurl.
Whispers of spring in the crisp, cool air,
Dreams awaken, a joyful affair.

Pumpkin fields glow like lanterns bright,
Echoes of laughter filling the night.
Candied apples and stories shared,
In autumn's grip, our spirits bared.

Fires crackle, warmth in the air,
With every glance, love is laid bare.
As the stars blanket the harvest moon,
Dreams of springtime return all too soon.

In this season, hope is reborn,
A reminder of blooms amidst the worn.
Embracing change, we find our song,
In dreams of spring, where we all belong.

Antlered Cadence at Dawn

Antlers rise against the sky,
A chorus of the wild nearby.
Morning spills its golden hue,
As nature dances, fresh and new.

Winds whisper tales of ancient lore,
While footsteps blend on forest floor.
In the chorus, spirits soar high,
Embracing joy, as moments fly.

Ribbons of light weave through the trees,
Painting shadows with gentle ease.
The heartbeat of the day unfolds,
In vibrant hues of greens and golds.

Celebrate the dawn's debut,
With every heartbeat, bright and true.
In laughter's echo, life's refrain,
We find our joy once again.

Sighs of the Late Autumn

Leaves flutter down in golden grace,
Whispers of change in every place.
The air is crisp, the skies are clear,
Embracing warmth as we draw near.

Pumpkins glow with candles bright,
Inviting tales in soft twilight.
Gather 'round, let stories flow,
As laughter dances, soft and low.

Scarves wrapped tight, we stroll beneath,
Nature's art, in silence, breath.
The world adorned in amber hues,
Late autumn sings in gentle tunes.

With every sigh, a memory made,
In fireside light, our worries fade.
In this season, hearts unite,
As stars emerge to greet the night.

Echoing through the Misty Vale

Through the vale where shadows play,
Echoes rise to greet the day.
Misty tendrils softly curl,
Leading whispers into whirl.

Laughter spills from hidden nooks,
Nature's canvas, storybooks.
In the silence, life takes flight,
Dancing freely, pure delight.

Colors blend in morning's hue,
As life awakens, fresh and true.
In the vale, our spirits sing,
Graced by joy that mornings bring.

Let the echoes guide our way,
Through the mist, we celebrate.
In this magic, hearts revive,
In every breath, we come alive.

A Lullaby of Soft Ferns

In shadows cast by ancient trees,
Soft ferns sway with gentle ease.
A lullaby of nature's tune,
Beneath the gaze of silver moon.

Crickets chirp in evening's calm,
While fireflies dance, a soothing balm.
The night unfolds in velvet hues,
As dreams emerge, our hearts peruse.

Rustling leaves, a secret choir,
Igniting in us quiet fire.
In the stillness, peace takes hold,
A timeless story, subtly told.

Let the ferns embrace the night,
In their grace, we find our light.
In this lullaby, spirits wend,
Together, we shall dream, my friend.

A Journey Through Wild Whispers

In the meadows, laughter swirls,
Dancing petals, bright as pearls.
Children's voices fill the air,
Joyous spirits everywhere.

Sunbeam kisses on the streams,
Nature hums, embracing dreams.
With each step, a new delight,
Stars await in velvet night.

Basketfuls of blooms unfold,
Stories of the earth retold.
Gentle breezes, whispers play,
Guiding hearts, come out and stay.

Here, together, hand in hand,
Magic flows across the land.
Laughter, love, and music's grace,
A journey through this perfect place.

The Language of Leaves

Rustling secrets in the trees,
Whispers carry on the breeze.
Golden hues kiss earth's embrace,
Summer's warmth, a sweetened pace.

Leaves applaud as breezes dance,
Nature's rhythm, a lively trance.
Colors mingle in delight,
Creating joy from morning light.

Every flutter tells a tale,
Songs of nature, soft and pale.
Underneath the canopy,
We find the roots of harmony.

Gathered here with hearts so free,
In the shade of the old tree.
With each leaf, a festive cheer,
In the language of the year.

Singsong of Celestial Glades

Through the glades, the soft winds sing,
Joyful notes that life can bring.
Light cascades from above, so bright,
Casting shadows with pure delight.

Gentle streams weave tales of old,
Whispers of the brave and bold.
In every flower's vivid hue,
A painted story, fresh and new.

Festive echoes fill the air,
Nature's concert, beyond compare.
Gather 'round, and let us sway,
In this dance, we'll find our way.

Moonlight's grace, a tender guide,
Leads us softly to the tide.
Together here, let spirits soar,
In the glades, forevermore.

The Invisible Orchestra of Nature

In shadows deep, the music flows,
With melodies the heart well knows.
Crisp leaves rustle, a gentle clap,
Nature's tune in every lap.

Birds compose the sunny scores,
While water skips on grassy shores.
With each note, the world ignites,
A festive rhythm that excites.

Join the dance of hidden sounds,
Feel the joy that nature bounds.
From soft whispers to thunderous roars,
A symphony that ever soars.

In harmony, all life takes part,
An orchestra that lifts the heart.
Together, let our spirits rise,
In nature's light, beneath the skies.

The Quiet Pulse of the Thicket

In the thicket where whispers sing,
Leaves shimmer bright, a joyous ring.
Each rustle tells a tale of cheer,
Nature's heart beats softly here.

Sunlight filters through the green,
Casting spells of gold between.
With every step, the beauty flows,
A tapestry of life that glows.

Birds take flight with jubilant cries,
Painting the canvas of summer skies.
In this realm where laughter dwells,
The thicket's pulse, a story tells.

With every breath, the world feels new,
A festive spirit bidding adieu.
To all that's gray, embrace the light,
In the thicket's arms, all feels right.

Echoes of Verdant Elegance

Beneath the boughs of emerald cheer,
Where flowers bloom and skies are clear.
The air is sweet with nature's song,
In this place, we all belong.

Echoes dance on gentle breeze,
Whispered secrets through the trees.
Celebrate the vibrant sway,
As life unfolds in bright array.

The brook bubbles, a laughter shared,
With every ripple, joy prepared.
In the elegance of verdant grace,
Festive hearts find their embrace.

Under a quilt of starlit dreams,
The night weaves whispers, soft as beams.
In every shadow, light will bloom,
As nature's beauty fills the room.

The Dance of Lively Shadows

As twilight falls, the shadows play,
In hues of gold and soft decay.
Amidst the trees, the spirits twirl,
In a lively dance, their joy unfurl.

Glow of lanterns, flicker bright,
Inviting all to join the night.
Feet find rhythm in the grass,
Where laughter echoes, moments pass.

In every sway, a story spun,
Under the gaze of the setting sun.
The night unfolds with vibrant glee,
As shadows weave their mystery.

With every heartbeat, smiles expand,
We celebrate this festive land.
In the dance of shadows, let us roam,
In joyous circles, we find our home.

Muses of the Green Expanse

In fields of green, the muses soar,
In every corner, life's galore.
The daisies nod, the breezes flow,
With every whisper, joy will grow.

A canvas brushed in vivid hues,
In nature's art, we find our muse.
Each flower sways with gentle grace,
Bringing smiles to every face.

Laughter dances on the wind,
In harmony, our hearts rescind.
The green expanse, a playground wide,
In festive spirit, we confide.

With open hearts, we chase the light,
Embracing moments, pure delight.
For in this world so lush and grand,
The muses guide us, hand in hand.

The Poetry of Prance

In the meadow, laughter rings,
Colors dancing, joy it brings.
Spirits soaring, hearts in flight,
Celebrate through day and night.

Underneath the vibrant sky,
Friends and cheer, the time goes by.
Songs of fortune, tales unfold,
Joy in every heart, behold!

Candles glow with soft delight,
Twinkling stars wink in the night.
Hands together, voices raise,
In this moment, love ablaze.

Glorious shimmers, every glance,
Life's a tapestry of dance.
With each heartbeat, laughter's call,
Together we shall have it all.

Morning's Breath in the Clearing

Sunrise whispers through the trees,
Rustling softly in the breeze.
Golden light on dew-kissed grass,
A brand new day is here at last.

Birds are singing, bright and clear,
Nature's choir, music near.
Joyful echoes through the glade,
In this moment, dreams invade.

Petals open, colors bloom,
Sweet perfume dispels the gloom.
With each breath, the spirit wakes,
In this warmth, my heart remakes.

Every heartbeat, every sigh,
Beneath the wide and open sky.
Particles of love-fueled grace,
In morning's breath, we find our place.

Notes from the Glade

Whispers weave through ancient pine,
Gentle breezes, oh so fine.
In the glade where shadows play,
Nature sings the joy of day.

Crickets chirp, the sunset glows,
Underneath, the river flows.
With each note, the soul takes flight,
In harmony with day and night.

Fern and flower, side by side,
Life's a journey, no need to hide.
Echoes of merriment abound,
In this sacred space, we're found.

Sparkling laughter, feet in dance,
Every moment a sweet chance.
Together here, we find our muse,
In the glade, our minds we lose.

The Rhythm of Thistle and Thorn

Dancing shadows, wild and free,
Nature hums her melody.
In the thistle, beauty grows,
Guarded secrets, life bestows.

Underneath the light of sun,
Join in harmony, everyone.
Thorny paths can still bring cheer,
In the laughter, hold us near.

Moments shared, let worries fade,
In the glow, our hearts cascade.
With each step, the world's alive,
Through the thistle, love will thrive.

Celebrate this wondrous song,
Where the brave and kind belong.
In every twist and turn we trace,
Together we shall find our place.

Rhythms of the Rustling Leaves

In autumn's dance, leaves take flight,
Colors flash in the waning light.
Laughter swirls on the crisp cool air,
Joyful hearts gather everywhere.

Underneath the golden trees,
Nature hums in mellifluous ease.
Bonfires crackle, shadows play,
A symphony at close of day.

With every gust, the branches sway,
Festive spirits come out to play.
Songs of old drift on the breeze,
Life unfolds with such sweet ease.

Together we share, hands entwined,
Memories cherished, spirits aligned.
In rhythm with the rustling leaves,
We celebrate all that life weaves.

A Stag's Soliloquy

In moonlit glades, the stag stands tall,
Whispers echo, his voice a call.
Majestic grace, he claims the night,
With antlers wide and eyes so bright.

Around him dance the stars above,
Nature's chorus sings of love.
Each step made on the velvet ground,
In every heartbeat, magic found.

With echoes of the forest's song,
He wanders where the wild belong.
His solitude, a cherished cheer,
In festive woods, he has no fear.

For in the stillness, joy abounds,
In whispered breaths, the heart resounds.
The stag, a guardian of the night,
Brings forth the magic, pure delight.

Reflections in the Dew

Softly blink at dawn's first light,
Dewdrops glisten, a sparkling sight.
Nature's gems on blades of green,
A wondrous world, so fresh, serene.

In the hush, whispers of the day,
Promises wrapped in soft array.
Each droplet holds a tale to tell,
Of fleeting moments, all is well.

As sunlight kisses, shadows flee,
Inviting laughter, wild and free.
Children play in fields anew,
Chasing dreams, like droplets, too.

In every gleam, a story swirls,
Reflections play as life unfurls.
With every step, joy's sweet embrace,
We celebrate this sacred space.

Enchanted Footprints at Dusk

As twilight bows, the path aglow,
Footprints mark where dreamers go.
With every step, a soft beacon,
In shadows rich, the night's begun.

The air is filled with songs of cheer,
Enchanted whispers, close and near.
Lantern lights flicker, hearts aligned,
In every gathering, joy we find.

Beneath the stars, hand in hand,
Together we weave a magic band.
The world transformed in dusky hue,
With laughter shared, our spirits grew.

So let us wander, paths unknown,
With every step, love has grown.
In enchanted footprints, we celebrate,
As dusk descends, it's never too late.

Dance of the Silent Hoof

In a glade where shadows play,
Hooves tap lightly on the way,
Stars twinkle in the night sky,
While whispers of the breeze sigh.

A moonlit path, we step and glide,
Nature's rhythm, side by side,
Laughter blends with rustling leaves,
In this night, the heart believes.

With every leap, the world ignites,
Colors spark in joyful flights,
Hoofbeats echo, soft and sweet,
In this dance, our spirits meet.

Under stars, we laugh and spin,
A festive joy will now begin,
Together in this silent room,
We're alive in nature's bloom.

Melodies of the Meadow

In fields where daisies gently sway,
The sun paints gold upon the day,
A symphony of breezes sings,
As nature calls with vibrant wings.

Butterflies in colors bright,
Dance on petals, pure delight,
Bees a-whirr in sweet repose,
In this land where laughter grows.

The brook hums softly, murmurs sweet,
A harmony beneath our feet,
With every step, the joy expands,
As we join in with nature's bands.

In the meadow's warm embrace,
We celebrate this sacred place,
A festive spirit shared with all,
In melodies that rise and fall.

Twilight Call of Graceful Shadows

As twilight drapes the earth in blue,
Shadows dance and dreams come true,
Stars awaken, one by one,
In this magic, we have fun.

The night unfolds like velvet lace,
While laughter wanders, finds its place,
Cool breezes bring a whispered cheer,
In this dusk, all hearts draw near.

Fireflies twinkle with delight,
Guiding us through soft, serene night,
With every flicker, spirits rise,
Underneath the starlit skies.

Together here, not far apart,
We celebrate with all our heart,
In shadows woven, dreams will grow,
A festive dance in twilight's glow.

Harmony in the Hollow

In the hollow where the willows sway,
Music plays throughout the day,
Joyful sounds fill the air,
As laughter spins in a carefree flare.

Children's voices ring like chimes,
Echoing through the fragrant limes,
With each note, our spirits soar,
In this place, we long for more.

The crackling fire sends sparks high,
We share our dreams beneath the sky,
Together we weave tales of old,
In harmony, our hearts behold.

As the night wraps us in its song,
We know here is where we belong,
In the hollow, festive and bright,
We celebrate the magic of night.

Artistry of the Quiet Grove

In the grove where shadows play,
Colors dance in warm array,
The laughter of the leaves so bright,
Whispers of joy in morning light.

Petals twirl in gentle sway,
Nature's canvas on display,
Every hue a story told,
In the quiet, pure and bold.

Birds alight with songs to share,
Melodies weave through fragrant air,
Bubbles burst with laughter sweet,
In this grove, our hearts do meet.

Every step a joyous beat,
Harmony beneath our feet,
In the artistry divine,
Festive spirits intertwine.

When Nature's Harp Strikes

When the dawn begins to glow,
Nature's harp begins to flow,
Strings of light and shadows blend,
In this moment, all transcend.

Gentle breeze, a soft caress,
Woven dreams in sweet finesse,
Notes of laughter lift the day,
In this symphony, we sway.

Crickets chirp a lively tune,
Underneath the watchful moon,
Fireflies dance, a twinkling show,
When Nature's harp begins to blow.

In this magic, hearts ignite,
Music flows from day to night,
Every sound a joyful spark,
In nature's love, we leave our mark.

Beneath the Silvered Birch

Beneath the silvered birch we lay,
Counting stars that greet the day,
Stories whispered on the breeze,
Wrapped in moments such as these.

Dancing light through branches streams,
Capturing our playful dreams,
Joyous laughter, bright and clear,
In this grove, we hold our cheer.

Rustling leaves in stories old,
Memories in whispers told,
Every flicker of the night,
Brings our hearts a pure delight.

Beneath the silvered birch we find,
Magic threads that weave and bind,
In nature's arms, our spirits soar,
Festive echoes, evermore.

The Whispering Breeze

The whispering breeze in balmy nights,
Carries joy and pure delights,
Crickets sing, the stars align,
In the dark, we brightly shine.

Moonlight dances on the ground,
Every heartbeat, every sound,
Reflects the joy of life so free,
In this moment, you and me.

Gentle winds with secrets call,
Underneath the trees so tall,
Every rustle, every gleam,
In this night, we share a dream.

So let the breeze guide our way,
As we linger, laugh, and sway,
In the warmth of nature's song,
In this festivity, we belong.

Fleeting Shadows in the Hollow

In the glen where laughter sways,
Fleeting shadows dance and play.
Beneath the moon's gentle glow,
Joyful hearts bask in the flow.

Lanterns twinkle in the night,
Chasing dreams, they take their flight.
Each whisper carried by the breeze,
Magic spun among the trees.

Songs of old fill the air,
Memories linger everywhere.
As twilight fades, the stars appear,
A tapestry of light so clear.

Let us savor every cheer,
In the hollow, friends are near.
With each moment, laughter grows,
In fleeting shadows, love still glows.

The Graceful Wanderer

With every step, a story blooms,
The graceful wanderer resumes.
Through fields of gold and skies of blue,
Adventures call, forever new.

Dancing in the softest light,
Chasing dreams that take to flight.
Laughter echoes through the trees,
Like whispers carried by the breeze.

In every corner, joy awaits,
A symphony of open gates.
As seasons shift and friendships grow,
In simple moments, love will flow.

So come along this winding road,
Where happiness is freely strode.
Hand in hand, we'll weave our way,
The graceful wanderer at play.

Woodland Whispers

Deep within the leafy dome,
Woodland whispers find their home.
Secrets shared with rustling leaves,
In this haven, the heart believes.

Crickets sing a lovely tune,
Beneath the watchful, silver moon.
Fireflies flicker, sparks of glee,
A dance of light, wild and free.

Each path leads to wonderland,
In nature's clasp, we take a stand.
Every laugh, a note to soar,
In woodland whispers, spirits explore.

Join the circle, lose the grind,
In its embrace, true peace we find.
Hand in hand, we weave the night,
With woodland whispers, hearts take flight.

Serenities Among the Pines

Among the pines where breezes sigh,
Serenities draw nigh.
Golden rays filter through the trees,
Bringing warmth with gentle ease.

Candles flicker in the shade,
As friendships bloom, unafraid.
Laughter mingles with the air,
Joyful memories to share.

Stars awaken in the dusk,
A tapestry of dreams and trust.
Nature's canvas, bold and bright,
Together here, our souls take flight.

In stillness, peace ignites the night,
A symphony of pure delight.
So gather close, let spirits rise,
In serenities 'neath the skies.

The Veil Between Worlds

In twilight's glow, the shadows dance,
A whispering breeze, a fleeting chance.
Bright lanterns flicker, spirits cheer,
Together we gather, joyfully near.

The stars above like sparks ignite,
A tapestry woven in silken night.
We share our laughter, we share our dreams,
In this enchanted realm, nothing's as it seems.

The veil grows thin, as magic swells,
With stories told, the heart compels.
Each heartbeat echoes, a rhythm so sweet,
In harmony's arms, our souls meet.

With each embrace, friendships delight,
A carnival spirit ignites the night.
Underneath the moon, we twirl and sway,
In a festival dream, we dance and play.

An Amble Through the Thicket

Beneath the boughs where colors gleam,
A pathway winds, like a vivid dream.
With laughter shared, we pick our pace,
In nature's arms, we find our place.

The sunbeams play, a golden hue,
Where petals blush in morning dew.
Birds serenade, their songs so clear,
In this wild embrace, we shed our fear.

Each turn reveals a secret glade,
Where memories wait, and joys cascade.
With every step, the world unfolds,
A tapestry woven in stories told.

Together we wander, hearts aligned,
Through thicket's charm, our spirits entwined.
In this playful realm, we gleefully roam,
In the forest's heart, we find our home.

Secrets of Marshland Stillness

Amidst the reeds where whispers flow,
A tranquil hush, the world moves slow.
Reflections shimmer, soft and bright,
In marshland's calm, we find our light.

The dragonflies flit with jeweled grace,
A dance of life in this sacred space.
With secrets held, the waters gleam,
In their quiet depths, we dare to dream.

The twilight calls, as shadows blend,
With heartbeats matched, and spirits mend.
We share our stories, ancient and new,
In this stillness, we feel the true.

As fireflies glow and laughter swells,
A symphony of nature, magic dwells.
Together we forge this gentle bliss,
In marshland's heart, find endless kiss.

Beneath the Oak's Ancient Wisdom

Beneath the oak, where ages rest,
A gathering place, our hearts are blessed.
With leaves like whispers, secrets shared,
Together we weave dreams, fully prepared.

The branches sway in the evening breeze,
With tales of old, the past appease.
In this embrace, we learn and grow,
With laughter's echo, time seems to slow.

Around the trunk, like children divine,
We plant our hopes, our spirits align.
In the shade, where stories thrive,
Beneath the oak, we truly live.

As dusk descends, a golden hue,
We celebrate life, and all that's new.
Embracing the night, in joy unconfined,
Under the oak, our hearts intertwine.

Whispers of the Woodland

In dappled light, the leaves do dance,
With laughter bright, a merry chance.
The brook sings low, a gentle tune,
As sunbeams weave through shades of June.

The creatures join, a lively throng,
Each note they share a vibrant song.
The fox prances, the deer do sway,
In this enchanted, joyful play.

A whisper winds through branches high,
Like secrets held in twilight's sigh.
The air is sweet with blooms that cheer,
A fest of nature, year by year.

With every step, the earth's delight,
In woodland paths, the heart takes flight.
Each shadow hides a joyful grin,
A world where simply bliss begins.

Echoes of the Antlered Heart

Beneath the sky, a canvas bright,
The antlers gleam in golden light.
The drums of joy beat in the air,
While whispers weave through lovers' flair.

The starlit night, a velvet cloak,
As laughter spreads, a cheerful croak.
The owls join in, a soft refrains,
In moonlit realms, where magic reigns.

The deer step forth, with reverent grace,
Each heartbeat echoes in this place.
The forest hums with vibrant cheer,
As nature's kin draw ever near.

In meadows paused, the moments glean,
With every breath, a love serene.
These echoes linger, soft and sweet,
In every joy the heart may meet.

Serenade of the Forest Glade

Where shadows play and sunlight gleams,
The forest whispers ancient dreams.
In glades adorned with blooms so bright,
The echoes swirl, a pure delight.

The brooklet's song, a crystal chime,
In rhythm soft, it drifts through time.
With petals falling, colors blend,
In nature's arms, we find our friend.

The crickets hum their twilight song,
While starlight twinkles, pure and strong.
Each rustling leaf invites a sigh,
A serenade beneath the sky.

The day grows old, the night awakes,
In every heartbeat, laughter shakes.
In unity, the spirits glide,
A dance of joy, in glades we bide.

Lullaby Beneath the Canopy

Beneath the leaves, a world unfolds,
With stories rich, and dreams retold.
The gentle breeze, a soft caress,
A lullaby, the heart's own dress.

The stars peek through, like diamonds bright,
In whispered tones, they share the night.
The owls call out, a sweet refrain,
Their voices twine in nature's gain.

The nightingale sings soft and low,
As time drifts on, a tranquil flow.
The shadows dance upon the ground,
In magic's hold, we're softly bound.

With every sigh, the darkness hums,
The woodlands thrive, the joy becomes.
In slumber deep, our dreams take flight,
A lullaby beneath the night.

Nightfall's Quiet Mantra

As twilight drapes in hues of gold,
Whispers of joy in the air unfold.
Laughter dances on the evening breeze,
Stars peek out from the slumbering trees.

Candles flicker in a cozy glow,
Soft melodies drift, sweet and low.
The world wraps in a gentle embrace,
A moment of peace in this magical place.

Children's giggles float with delight,
While shadows weave dreams in the night.
Joyous hearts join in a song,
Together we thrive, where we all belong.

So let the night weave its gentle thread,
With festive hopes, our hearts are fed.
In the stillness, let our spirits soar,
Nightfall's quiet mantra, forevermore.

The Forest's Silent Rhyme

Beneath the branches, where secrets dwell,
Nature's laughter, a soft-spoken bell.
Each rustle tells of stories spun,
In the heart of the woods, where dreams run.

Crisp leaves crisp underfoot, a delight,
Colors ablaze in the warm sunlight.
A gathering of friends, smiles so wide,
In the forest's embrace, we joyfully reside.

Wildflowers bloom in a vibrant dance,
Each petal a note, a sweet chance.
Echoes of peace, in every breeze,
The forest's silent rhyme, puts hearts at ease.

Celebrate together, hand in hand,
As we wander through this enchanting land.
Beneath a canopy, our spirits entwined,
In nature's rhythm, the joyous aligned.

Sprites of the Timbered Grove

Amidst the trees where the fairies play,
Laughter sparkles in the light of day.
Tiny wings flutter in carefree flight,
Sprites of the grove dancing in delight.

Sunbeams weave through the emerald leaves,
Magic flows in the air that deceives.
The forest alive with a symphony sweet,
Whispers and giggles beneath our feet.

Mushrooms sprout in a playful row,
In this enchanted realm, imagination flows.
With every glance, wonder unfolds,
Stories of adventure in silence retold.

Gather near, let your worries cease,
Join in the dance, find your release.
In this timbered grove, where dreams arrive,
Together we bask, and feel so alive.

Paws upon the Earth

Little paws tread softly on the ground,
In the glade where laughter is found.
Tiny creatures, with joy in each leap,
Embrace the night in a festive sweep.

Mirthful chirps fill the amber sky,
As twinkling lights wink and sigh.
Creatures gather, a lively throng,
In the heart of nature, we all belong.

Moonlit paths where magic flows,
A journey of joy, where love grows.
With every step, new tales we weave,
Paws upon the earth, together we believe.

So let the evening's festivities bloom,
In our hearts, let happiness loom.
For in this moment, as night unfurls,
We find our bliss—our own little worlds.

Song of the Gentle Grazer

In fields of green with flowers bright,
Gentle grazers bask in light.
Their laughter dances with the breeze,
Nature sings in perfect ease.

The sunlit days bring joy anew,
With skies adorned in every hue.
They twirl and leap, so free and bold,
Stories of warmth and cheer unfold.

Among the oaks so grand and wise,
They share secrets with the skies.
With every step, they paint the day,
In a festive, joyous ballet.

As twilight falls, the world takes pause,
Together they stand, just because.
A gentle song, a heart's delight,
In the magic of summer night.

Dawn's Embrace in the Clearing

Dawn awakens with golden rays,
In the clearing, peace conveys.
Laughter echoes through the glen,
A new day's song, again and again.

Mist drapes softly on the ground,
Nature whispers all around.
With jubilant hearts, we begin,
A dance of life, we're joining in.

The colors burst like fireworks bright,
Each hue a spark, pure delight.
As the sun climbs, we feel so free,
Celebrating all that's meant to be.

In this embrace, the world feels right,
Under the canvas of morning light.
Together we share a joyous cheer,
In the dawning of a brand new year.

Songbirds and Silhouettes

Songbirds chirp a playful tune,
Beneath the gaze of the glowing moon.
In shadows dance the silhouettes,
A festival joy no one forgets.

With every flap, their spirits soar,
They flutter around, forevermore.
In the soft glow, they spin and glide,
Inviting hearts to join the ride.

Together we sway, so wild and free,
In the night's cool embrace, just you and me.
A tapestry of music unfolds,
With whispers of magic our hearts enfold.

As stars appear, we find our place,
In nature's wonder, a warm embrace.
We celebrate love, laughter, and light,
In this serene, enchanting night.

Starlit Serenades of the Glen

Under the canopy of twinkling stars,
The world feels close, despite the afar.
Each note carries a tale of grace,
In the glen, we find our place.

The serenade flows like gentle streams,
Woven with laughter and shared dreams.
With every strum, the night ignites,
Igniting happiness that delights.

Moonlit pathways call us near,
Unity blossoms, hearts sincere.
In our circle, joy does blend,
With starlight woven, we transcend.

As melody echoes through the night,
Every whisper, a spark of light.
Together we stand, forever blessed,
In the magic of starlit fest.

Harmony Among the Leaves

In golden light, the leaves embrace,
Laughter dances in the gentle space.
Colors twirl in the autumn's song,
Nature's joy where we all belong.

Breezes whisper secrets of cheer,
While sunlight beckons smiles near.
Leaves rustle softly, a sweet refrain,
Life's vibrant pulse we can't contain.

With every step, the earth will sway,
In this grand fest, we laugh and play.
Harmony flows in nature's breath,
A tapestry of life and death.

As twilight deepens, shadows blend,
The warmth of friendship will not end.
Under the canopy, dreams take flight,
Together, we bask in the fading light.

A Chorus of Starlit Hooves

Underneath the vast, twinkling skies,
A chorus of hooves brings joyous cries.
Stars pirouette in the velvet night,
Filling hearts with wonder and delight.

Galaxies twinkle, the rhythm's alive,
In harmony, the wild spirits thrive.
The moon keeps watch on this festive parade,
Where magic and melody serenade.

Fields awaken with every beat,
Nature dances, its pulse so sweet.
A symphony plays, the world's alive,
In this moment, together we thrive.

Echoing laughter fills the air,
Starlit memories beyond compare.
In the night's embrace, we all belong,
As the universe hums its timeless song.

In the Realm of Soft Shadows

Where lights flicker and shadows play,
In this realm, we wander and sway.
Dreams drift lightly on the breeze,
Whispers of laughter dance through the trees.

A tapestry woven with threads of light,
In the soft shadows, everything feels right.
Candles glow with a warmth so dear,
Each flame a beacon, drawing us near.

The air is rich with stories untold,
In hushed tones, these moments unfold.
With every glance, connections ignite,
In the soft shadows, hearts feel so bright.

As twilight deepens and stars start to gleam,
We share our wishes, we share our dreams.
In laughter and joy, we find our way,
Together we glow at the end of the day.

Moonlit Serenade of the Glen

Beneath the moon, the glen softly sighs,
As crickets perform their melodic cries.
Night blooms with magic and gentle grace,
In this serenade, we find our place.

Fireflies twinkle in a dance so bright,
Guiding our hearts through the velvet night.
Each step forward, a heartbeat in tune,
With nature's rhythm beneath the moon.

Laughter echoes through the whispering trees,
Carried on currents of cool midnight breeze.
Moments entwined like the stars up above,
In the serenade, we bask in love.

Here in the hush, our spirits unite,
The glen holds our secrets, our purest light.
As dawn breaks softly to end the show,
We carry the magic wherever we go.